2014

MW01613060

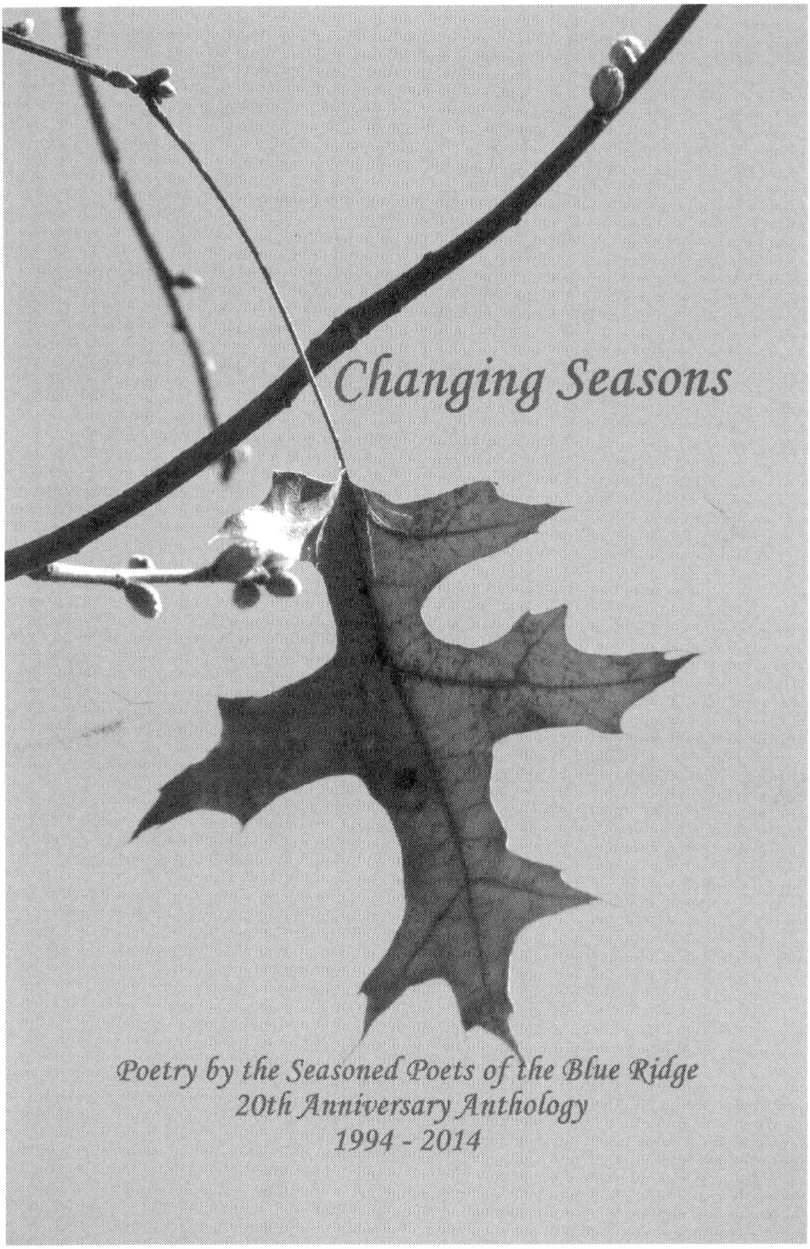

Changing Seasons

Poetry by the Seasoned Poets of the Blue Ridge
20th Anniversary Anthology
1994 - 2014

First Edition 2014

Current Members of the Seasoned Poets of the Blue Ridge with poetry in this eleventh anthology include: Elda Lepak, Laurabeth "Rusty" Breeding, Karen Heggen, Helen Palmer, Gwyneth Noble, and Beverly Bryan Russell.

Acknowledgment: The Seasoned Poets especially thank the following for the use of their facilities for meetings and/or readings over the past 20 years: First Methodist Church of Hendersonville, Carolina Village, the Flat Rock Village Hall, and the Henderson Country Library.

Cover and Book Design by: Elda Lepak
Photography by: Elda Lepak unless otherwise noted.

Available from Amazon.com, CreateSpace.com
and other retail outlets

Published by: Rivercrest Editions
                Hendersonville, NC

Printed in the United States of America by CreateSpace

ISBN-13: 978-1500647933
ISBN-10: 1500647934

Dedication

We dedicate *Changing Seasons*:

to the three poets whose poetry has kept them alive in our hearts:

> *Frances Miner Schneider (1904-2003)*
> *Hazel Herndon Fryer (1914-2003)*
> *Edith Pedersen (1922-2008)*

to the Henderson County Friends of the Library for their support of our poetry readings and other literary programs through the years...

to Helen van Boer, who taught the poetry class at Blue Ridge Community College that inspired the Seasoned Poets to form as a group...

to Laurabeth (Rusty) Breeding , Karen Heggen, Gwyneth Noble, and Helen Palmer, who have been writing together for twenty years.

We thank all who have contributed to our inspiration and longevity.

Foreword

Changing Seasons is a book of celebration of and reflection on the twenty years that we, the Seasoned Poets of the Blue Ridge, have enjoyed the many blessings of living in this unique section of Western North Carolina. Not native to this area, we have discovered its infinite beauties and the warmth of its inhabitants. We are proud to call it home.

Our group was formed from a class at Blue Ridge Community College, taught by Dr. Helen van Boer in 1994. Since then we have met weekly to discuss poets and poetry. We challenge ourselves with writing in different poetic forms and styles, and we present our efforts for admiration and criticism, first to the group and then to the wider public. We offer well-attended readings and encourage others in the community, young and old, to explore putting their own words on paper.

Through our twenty years together, we have mourned the deaths of three highly-valued and loved members, rallied around members who have lost their spouses, and supported others through patches of bad health. In the process we have become true friends. Though through individual perspectives, we all have embraced the changing seasons of our lives in so many ways. We hope that these poems will jog memories of similar moments in our readers' lives. Come celebrate with us the *Changing Seasons*!

Gwyneth Noble

Table of Contents

7

Seasoned Poets of the Blue Ridge

group photo by Peter Wollner

Current Poets

Back: Helen Palmer, Elda Lepak.
Middle: Gwyneth Noble, Karen Heggen
Front: Laurabeth "Rusty" Breeding.
Inset: Beverly Bryan Russell

Gwyneth Noble

Autumn

I find myself
mirroring Autumn,
a restless season
never being sure
of its direction.

Spring
is restless, too,
has a hard time
forgetting winter,
releasing itself
from its icy grasp.

But Autumn and I
remember summer. Sunny days,
warm winds,
soothing zephyrs
hesitating to leave.

Reluctantly
we bluster
into what lies ahead
scattering the leaves of life
until the inevitable
snows of winter
descend.

One World

When a loved one
is in the hospital
the world shrinks
to the size of that room.
The world IS the room.

The world is a bed
that moves up and down.
A chair, gained with enormous effort,
where an attempt to eat
tires one so
a return to bed is necessary.

The world becomes
a conglomerate of indignities,
where private urges
become public spectacles,
where a call for help
falls into a void.

I try to remember
the ever changing cast
that rotates through his world.
I want to humanize us,
get them on our team,
thank them, call them by name,
but new faces each day defeat me.

As I look out the window
I watch another world below.

Gwyneth Noble

A Summer Memory

It's not dark
nor truly light,
birds are saying
a long good-night.
Asleep in his chair,
book in hand
my husband dozes.
A TV band
drifts softly
from the house next door
I can't see
what I saw before
and close my book.
My tired eyes
welcome the sounds of night
untied.
The crunch of gravel
on unpaved road,
an airplane nearing
its next abode,
a neighbor's dog
whose frequent bark reminds me
of impending dark,
an annoying click
of rotating fan,
a memory of how
it all began.
What I wouldn't give to live just so.
A night on the porch two years ago.

Gwyneth Noble

The Pocket Knife

My husband was a careful man.
He was annoyingly perfect
in his carefulness,
almost Prussian
in his need for order.

He dressed immaculately for work,
shined his shoes
to mirrored perfection,
matched tie to suit,
breast pocket hanky folded just so.

He planned, he executed.
Studied outcomes.
Did not take chances.
Could be counted on
for thoughtful opinions.

In retirement he knew
where all his belongings were.
Kept all his tools in shape.
Screw drivers and wrenches
hung, sized, above his work bench.

Gwyneth Noble

14

He always carried a pocket knife
for small emergencies.
To open a wine bottle,
slice cheese, tomatoes, bread
on an al fresco picnic,
sever an entangling string,
liberate a fish,
dig out a troublesome weed.

As he aged
he began to lose things.
A cherished diamond ring.
What bothered him even more
was his favorite pocket knife.

Yesterday
I gave his no longer needed
reclining chair to a friend.
As his chair left the house
an opened pocket knife dropped
from some recess.

Grateful tears fell
for the huge gift I had received
from my small generosity.

Gwyneth Noble

Dog Is Love

Casey throws herself
in front of me,
blocks my hurried steps,
exposing her soft underbelly
to harried hands.
How does she know
I need a break?
I sit down beside her,
stroke her silky fur,
whisper quiet words,
find solace in the act.
Things will be all right, I tell her.

Photo by Gwyneth Noble

A Fashion Statement

Some dogs are born
to wear scarves.
Goldens and Labs
come immediately to mind,
exhibit a *je ne sais quoi*
suited for any engagement,
formal or informal.
They're ready.

Casey returned from the spa
uneasily wearing
a pink, yellow and green figured scarf
of chickens and eggs.
Like a vertically-challenged person
wearing a large hat tied under the chin
she is dwarfed
by its crisp jauntiness,
uneasy with the persona
it implies.

Within an hour
I find her scarf
hanging on a bush outside.

Gwyneth Noble

17

A Cautionary Tale

(What I Did On My Winter Vacation)

An invitation to live free
        in a condo by the sea
          sent a siren song to me.
My little dog and I
        packed our bags and said *goodbye.*
        We never even questioned why.
The condo rules contained errata.
        Little dogs, persona non grata.
        My naiveté ultimata.
So now I've learned, though very old,
        No longer smart, no longer bold,
        There's far worse things than being cold.

Gwyneth Noble

The Placid Gulf

is turbulent today.
Overnight storms
have stirred the pot
and brought it to a rolling boil.
The color has soured
with the bitter winds,
suggesting an acrid taste,
an unappetizing color
in contrast
to yesterday's blue.

Waves that earlier lapped ashore
beat angrily on the beach,
crash into each other
with thunderous sounds.
Bathers avoid the cauldron.
Two brave souls
walk the beach at a slant,
spin crazily with the wind
as sand cuts their legs.

Gwyneth Noble

The Impressionist

With the rigidity of
a classically-trained pianist
committed to the rigors
of lines and spaces
I listen in amazement and awe
as the young jazz pianist
exhibits his artistry.
The piano stretches to meet his demands,
lights up to comply with his mastery.
The shading is complex.
A walking bass, an unexpected trill,
pounding chords that turn delicate.
Syncopation throws an unexpected freshness
into the melody that weaves its way in and out
in a fashion only he can hear.
Just when you think it's lost forever
it reclaims its territory
in a minor mode
with a thrilling glissando
that sets it back on track.
There is a special genius in his fingers.

How I yearn to have the skill and courage
to color outside the lines!

Gwyneth Noble

Anne Boleyn

(Celebrated in Ceramics)

My face has been crafted
by skillful hands.
It's not really my face.
Not one I would recognize
if I caught a glimpse of myself
in a tiny window or
the small shard of glass
I called my mirror.
My features look small.
Pinched.
Not how I felt when
I threw back my head
and laughed lustily
as Henry threw me
over his shoulder
and carried me off to bed.
How powerful I felt...
for a time.
Until my face didn't satisfy,
my body didn't produce.
And the axe
altered
my face
forever.

Gwyneth Noble

Still Life With Spiders

Spiders demand attention
in the fall.
These Belgian lace makers have
stitched the burning bushes together,
created a doily to conceal the fading roses.
It's an old-fashioned appeal
reminiscent of tidy parlors in times past,
everything Grandma covered with a hand-fashioned
bit of thread.
Often the webs catch leaves
suspending them before my windows,
twisting and turning
like a Calder mobile.
Sometimes a hapless moth
is entwined,
providing a focal point,
an ephemeral wrap,
that, Cristo-like,
will be gone in the morning.

Gwyneth Noble

A More Orderly World Than Ours

About a foot from the garden wall
I set a plant to thrive.
Several days later, to my chagrin,
I found it no longer alive.

From under the pot a new world unfolded,
a cosmos of ants I'd uncovered,
frantically circling a mound in the middle
around which they nervously hovered.

Their moment of panic was over in seconds.
A phalanx of soldiers convened.
With martial precision two lines quickly formed
and order returned to the scene.

The mound disappeared in spectacular fashion.
Each ant seemed to answer a call
and bore his great burden with no hesitation,
each carrying an egg to the wall.

My drama was ended.
Serenity reigned.
Not a trace of catastrophe
even remained.

Gwyneth Noble

Past Glories

The whirligig on the gatepost
no longer spins.
His rotted sides
belie the hopeful fisherman
that deftly twirled fish and pole
years ago.
He is a travesty of himself.
The ravages time has imposed
make him impossible to admire
but there's still a sturdiness of purpose
in his weathered body.
Surprisingly his fundamental shape
is intact.
His hat still sits
at a jaunty angle,
the remnant of a smile
lingers on his damaged face.

How can I remove him?
I have looked in the mirror.

Gwyneth Noble

The Road Not Traveled

My sweet potato
aspires to more.
Does not wish to be
mashed with orange juice,
weighed down with marshmallows
and presented as a delicacy.
Nor does it dream
to be boiled in hot butter
and brown sugar,
then almost ignored
as a minor accompaniment
on the holiday table.

My sweet potato
has chosen another route.
Tender tendrils shoot out
from its leathery case.
Winding green arms
thrust upward,
embrace a new aesthetic.
A feast for the eyes
not the stomach emerges,
lingers on one's senses
long after the gustatory feast
is over.

Gwyneth Noble

Apres le Deluge

I'm shedding twenty years
of papers, cards and letters
in the basement.
Push has come to shove.
A flood
has captured my attention
in the basement.
I must dispose of things I love.

A cursory glance
at things gone musty.
The awful distancing
from what has mold.
Why does the odor
not repel me?
I know it's just a sign
of what's grown old.

I throw things carelessly.
The pile grows deep.
All these fine offerings
from those who love me,
I want to weep.
I try to keep a few mementos.
What should I throw out? What to keep?

Yet duty bids me to continue.
No way appears to show me how.
I'm losing twenty years of history
in the basement.
There's just no way of stopping now.

Gwyneth Noble

Early Risers

Crows provide
visual and aural accompaniment
to the unfolding pastoral scene,
their constant raucous cries annoying,
yet somehow comforting.

Another flock
taunts from across the lake.
A cloud of brown birds chatter through,
leaving in their wake
a deep silence.

It's only six A.M., in fact,
and human cohorts blissfully asleep
have yet to harvest daily cares,
their burdens still to reap.
But I,

I welcome others who rise early
and commence giving
evidence of those of us
already up,
engaged in living.

Gwyneth Noble

Laurabeth "Rusty" Breeding

Rusty Reflects: photo by Rusty Breeding

Reflection

Light hitting a non-absorbent surface
at a slant, continuing in the same direction
at a reversed angle, science says,
observed when a lens intersects its trajectory.

Reflection shines an internal light,
a poet says. The angles of view can be many,
the slant, at the poet's discretion.
A poet's reflection can move
backward or forward
and carries a charge of emotion.

Gumption

Some people just have gumption
while other people lack it.
Is it fair to make assumption
that you must get up, attack it?

I think we can agree
that for the less than gallant hearted
the problem seems to be
in getting up and getting started.

They say it's in the mind,
though that is undefined
and must be intertwined
with muscle tone departed.

We can weigh the pro and con,
classify, justify or magnify it,
deliberate and contemplate upon,
or we can simply sit and versify it.

Laurabeth "Rusty" Breeding

A First

That ball of fluff I chanced to see
huddled on a fallen tree
proved not what it was thought to be.
What twist of fate dropped luck on me?

Can explanation come from math
how random path can intersect with path?
A mystery that needn't elicit wrath
considering the fortune that one hath.

I thought at first that bunny rabbit
had made this spot its usual habit
where no fox was like to grab it
nor random arrow ever stab it.

I saw that ball of fluff uncurl.
Its color was a shade of pearl.
A long tail started to unfurl.
Surprise! Surprise! My first white squirrel.

Photo by Karen Heggen

Laurabeth "Rusty" Breeding

Remembering the Sky

I miss the stars.
Mountains lift the horizon
forty-five degrees on all sides.
Encircling trees rise even higher;
their overhanging boughs
noose the sky into a narrow window.
Light of a full moon sifts through the trees,
dappling a patchwork where it falls.

I remember Orion with the three-star belt,
the Big and Little Dippers, the North Star,
Andromeda, Cassiopeia, the Pleiades.
What a wide open world it was then.
The Northern Lights ran a chill down the spine,
not to mention the fingers and toes,
as we stood in the snow watching.

Nights in Australia, I searched for the Southern Cross.
Over the southern sea the atmosphere so clear,
I remember, that the whole heavens
stood out in three dimensions.

Now, no awe in the slim slice of sky.
One's lucky to see a shooting star.

Boughs noose the sky - photo by Laurabeth "Rusty" Breeding
Laurabeth "Rusty" Breeding

A Texas Tale

A prose poem

Mrs. LaRowe said when she was a baby, her folks moved across some part of Texas in a wagon. Early December, and cold, she didn't remember, they told her later. One evening at dark they came upon an abandoned house and decided to put up there 'til morning.

In the crumbling fireplace they made a fire. A rope bed built in the corner, they layered with blankets. Lantern blown out, parents and children snuggled down for the night.

Who heard it first, it doesn't matter – the scraping of scales on the hearth. Father lit the lantern with a match from his pants on the bedpost. In the flickering shadows he saw what he knew he would see: a floor writhing in rattlesnakes. Hibernating under the stones of the fireplace – warmth of the fire had brought them alive.

This story has a happy ending. The roof was low, the boards dry rotted. They tore a hole through the shingles, lifted the children, one by one, to the roof, hitched the horses, prancing, snorting the scent, and escaped in the night.

Laurabeth "Rusty" Breeding

March Lite

March swoops in like a murder of crows
with western winds and northern snows.

Like a child in a tantrum who's apt to fling
anything handy – that's March; it's spring.

Daffodils and crocus take an early chance
do-si-do the weather in a springtime dance.

Days will get warmer, nights will be cool.
March leaves announcing, "April Fool!"

Laurabeth "Rusty" Breeding

Taxing

Finances aren't that complicated
Don't know why I've waited – waited
Accumulated all the facts
It's time to do the income tax
    The forms are here from IRS
    I just have to sort this mess
    Enter wages, salaries, tips
    Otherwise the entry skips
Figure interest Schedule B
If this applies, do Part III
Wonder what the form intends
They list two parts for dividends
    Refunds, credits, leave this blank
    Where is the statement from the bank?
    Schedule D – gain or loss
    My eyes have now begun to cross
Read the rules, Page 23
Does anything apply to me?
Do the worksheet – 24
Complete the other form before
    Add amount Box 5, line 1
    Divide and enter half the sum
    Carry forward, minus, plus
    Compare with numbers previous
If 7 minus 8 is less
Check box labeled *No* or *Yes*
If this amount is zero, bigger
See line 20, that's your figure
    Things look good, I'm nearly done
    Turn the page – I've just begun!
    I haven't quit. Won't think of quitting
    Just leave it for a second sitting.

(Just to the Right of the Moon, 2002)

Laurabeth "Rusty" Breeding

Moon

In the style of Trees by Joyce Kilmer

I think that I shall never croon
a song as lovely as a moon.

A moon who finds celestial place
against the curtain of black space.

A moon whose face to God is bare,
whose silver beams are spread in prayer.

A moon who might in summer see
a silent scene or revelry.

A moon whose shining sparkles rain
and rivals snow upon the plain.

Poems are made – I've done my best.
Only a moon can tell the rest.

Laurabeth "Rusty" Breeding

Nelson Mandela
1918 – 2013

The airwaves pulse with praise
for a man who learned to forgive.
Millions of voices raise
in adoration and in grief.

Unlike the hermit prophets,
who chose isolation,
his years of forced confinement
rendered his simmering wrath to clarity,
broke the shackles, shattered the millstone,
released the energy for better use.

"We are all one nation," he declared.
The miracle is that people listened.

Laurabeth "Rusty" Breeding

Inspired by Tennyson's Quote

"I dipt into the future far as human eye could see"
from "Locksley Hall" by Tennyson.

I dipped into my memory
far as my inner eye could see
saw a vision of the past
things as they used to be.
Saw the carrier of commerce
behemoths of the rail
dropping down their mottled cargo
I heard the whistle wail.
Saw a busy railway station
felt the hustle of the throng
red capped porters shouting
carts of luggage pushed along.
Saw trains and ships of soldiers
saw trenches filled with mud
flying standards of the nations
as they spilled each other's blood.
Conflict after conflict
echoed round the world.
I watched in awe and wondered
if flags of battle ever will be furled.

Laurabeth "Rusty" Breeding

Blue Ghost Fireflies

(DuPont Forest – May)

We turned off our flashlights.
A crushed limestone path
illumined our way.
Not alone, we were in
the company of dozens.
Silence ruled.

Left and right they appeared –
floating stars, glowing
in the undergrowth, hovering,
slowly moving waves,
constantly alight.

In the darkness the pathway
mimicked the undulation,
challenging our balance.
Viewers in light clothing
were visible, dark ones
resembled posts and
ran the risk of collision.

The faceless became friends,
murmuring admiration
in a world that seemed to have
nothing stable to hold to.

Laurabeth "Rusty" Breeding

Southern Winter

Away up north in times gone by
the robin was our sign of spring.
Today is New Year's Day and I
aroused a flock of robins to take wing.

They circled round and settled down
where winter grass is green,
where seeds and grubs can still be found,
where horses had all summer been.

I wonder, will the robins go
when an Arctic front advances,
when the forecast is for snow,
or find a barn and take their chances.

Laurabeth "Rusty" Breeding

Inevitably

He thought that man was dogs' best friend
and ran to greet each car that passed.
One could predict the story's end,
but not which day would be his last.

So it is with humans, too,
our lives are one long race.
As many years become a few
we never know what we may face.

We may ponder what we've learned --
Have expectations been surpassed?
Are there credits we have earned?
Will it matter at the last?

We comfort in our memories made
in times that now are history.
Our hope is that all debts are paid
and we depart with dignity.

(First Place SilverArts Competition,
Henderson County, NC, 2013)

Laurabeth "Rusty" Breeding

Midnight Unrest

With apologies to Edgar Allan Poe

Once upon a midnight dreary
when my sunburned eyes were weary
of the evening television bore

    I clicked it off – there came a talking,
    as if it were a measured mocking,
    talking, talking, coming from the upper floor.

I knew there was no use in walking,
as I could be charged with stalking,
walking to the upper floor.

    So, I lay, my pillow blocking
    all the loud and raucous talking
    everything I heard and more.

Anything that could be shocking,
while my brain was gently rocking.
Eventually, I began to snore.

    In my dreams were ravens flocking,
    knights with falcons practiced hawking
    as they did in days of yore.

Then there came a violent knocking.
Startled, I sat up and gawking
heard the knocking on my motel door.

    Heard harsh words from the offended
    by nothing I could have intended.
    "Hey, you! Knock off that snore!"

Laurabeth "Rusty" Breeding

Download

Do you ever feel that the technical world
is pulling the rug from under your feet?
Just when you get their tangle uncurled
they tell you your program is obsolete.

So, you download another – their latest version,
then everything linked with it needs updating.
You feel like you're drowning in tech-talk immersion
with added frustration from Internet waiting.

What can we do to keep up the pace?
So many choices and all inter-connected.
What were the forces that unleashed this race?
And how did we get what we never expected?

Laurabeth "Rusty" Breeding

Generational Green

There's an Internet Forward you may have seen,
something described as "generational green."
It has circled for years and numberless miles
bringing each generation their own kind of smiles.

Brown paper bags changed to groceries in plastic –
Somebody thought this idea fantastic
for saving our trees and preserving our green
while plastic grows landfills, if you see what I mean.

Some kids rode their bikes, some walked to school,
but the next generation thought Mom's taxi was cool.
We carried our lunches in a bag or lunch box
or went home for lunch, a number of blocks.

We hung clothes on lines, carried in hampers;
we boiled cotton diapers; now they use Pampers.
Clothes were passed down from brother to brother,
some wore home-sewn, fashioned by Mother.

Very quickly things changed with large family needs;
machines in the kitchen or to cut grass and weeds.
The car became king, though it guzzled much gas;
air conditioning and heat are now expected en masse.

We old folk remember how we toughed out the times
that prompted these e-mail forwards and rhymes.
But before we begin our egos to puff,
remember 'twas we who bought all this stuff.

Laurabeth "Rusty" Breeding

Here's the Quandary

Here's the quandary:
    Did ever any thinker
        great or famous ever think
            of laundry?

Did the sages through the ages
    who pondered fowl and fishes
        and other things delicious
            ever ponder
                washing dishes?

Did any doctor (*witch* or *which*)
    Hottentot or Hindu
        ever have to
            wash a window?

Is there a shaman Cree or Sioux
    who can give to me or you
        a recipe with meaning
            that can cope with
                spring cleaning?

And the floors
    and the doors
    and the stairs
        and the chairs.......

Laurabeth "Rusty" Breeding

Helen Palmer

Housman Remembered

When I was one-and-sixty
      I heard no wise men speak.
I thought I'd heard it all before;
      No new news came this week.

I read each book as paradigm
      Of books I'd read before.
I heard each song with sad refrain
      And thought, *Oh, what a bore.*

But when I tried my wit on poems
      A flood of verse did pour
All those old thoughts returned to me
      Dressed up in metaphor.

I scarce could look at any flower
      Without a pen in hand.
Each day seemed fresh because I saw
      New footprints in the sand.

And I'm now one-and-eighty
      Still learning how to see.
The best of all those captured sights
      Create eternity.

(Jigsaw Puzzle, 1997, revised)

Journal

Seize the day
in words
on paper.

Seize each passing thought—
refrigerate them in the ice pack of words.

Seize each fickle emotion—
dress it up with lace and flowers
to parade down the aisle of memory.

Seize the sorrows of strangers
seen on the screen—
clothe them in tears of ink, soon dry.

Pack them in boxes
placed high on a shelf,
dust-laden, yellowed paper crumbling,
the *you* of *then*,
as wrinkled as a prune.

(The Taste of Waking, 2000)

Helen Palmer

Poetry Group

We sit at tables
linked like carbon atoms
but octagonal. We discuss
the moon landing retrospective,
fire under the earth,
French artists and model,
present and future trips to Europe.

Norman Rockwell's umpires
and game birds caught in golden flight
hang on the wall.

Our rolling chairs would allow us
to skateboard around the room,
if we dared,
but we sit,
pen in hand,
praying over scraps of paper.

(The Taste of Waking, 2000)

Helen Palmer

Many Hands Make Light Work
or The Myth of Sisyphus

Sisyphus was condemned
to roll a stone up a hill,
watch it fall back, trudge back down
and roll it back up--eternally.

We faced a similar dilemma--
moving the contents of a pallet
of three-inch river rock
in a wheelbarrow to a ditch.
Back and forth we went
and filled the area,
but still had what seemed
a mountain of rocks left.

Our neighbor took pity on us,
offered to put the remaining rocks in his truck
and deposit them at the top of the driveway
to use around flowerbeds.

So three adults and four children (ages 8 to 3)
tossed rocks into the truck,
then tossed them out, once on higher ground.
We made a sport of it,
a bucket brigade of rock tossers,
enjoying the heft of smooth rocks
and the well-earned dusty clothes.

The children had an impromptu game
and we had bonded with our neighbors.

The gods never had it so good.

Helen Palmer

The Fishermen

The neighbor children
found a fishing hole
on our cul-de-sac,

an inch-deep puddle
that forms
with every rain.

Two-year-old Noah,
just released from the ark,
stood hopefully on Mt. Ararat

with short stick, string attached
and who knows what bait
to lure the water bugs.

Would that I
could greet a flood
with such imagination.

Helen Palmer

51

Solace

I thought, *I'd like to have him*
preach at my funeral...
but not yet.

This service was for a man
whose family suffered
the long good-bye of Alzheimer's...

a tribute to the vibrant life
he led as soldier, engineer,
traveler, gardener, artist,
community theater actor,
loving father and husband.

This pruner of roses and
scourge of his neighbors' dandelions,
a man calm even when his daughter's
misstep on the gas pedal
took out a chunk of the family room,

was resurrected for us
by the loving words of his daughter
and a minister who had not met him.

Helen Palmer

Geriatric

I gaze at Katie,
our featherweight Siamese,
whose sharp bones remind me
that she's almost eighteen.

I listen for the ritual meow
repeated earnestly as she stalks
along the hallway when we are in bed,
the same sound she made when
playing with her sock toy, now lost.

I note the cat hair on the favorite
pillow where she takes her daily nap,
the small table we've placed
in front of the dryer where she eats,
to compensate for her inability
to jump high. We cater to her dietary whims,
as she seeks chicken this week,
bacon the next. I don't complain about
cleaning her pot twice a day.

I cherish her idiosyncrasies,
remind myself that she is just
a four-legged inhabitant
of our "rest home."

photo by Helen Palmer

Helen Palmer

Un-listed

An organized brain
I tried to maintain.
Tasks for the day
were filed away
in my memory store
but I'm sharp no more.

Though I tend to resist
a pen-and-paper list,
lists keep me aware:
of when I must be where;
of the letters I've sent;
to whom that book was lent;
of when I go for my hair;
or have a luncheon to share;
or when a payment is due.

Yet I haven't a clue
where the list went to!

Helen Palmer

54

Driving Lesson

All my usual routes are bumpy
as I drive about our town.
This one has two potholes, that one,
six storm drains to go around.

If perchance the bumps were smoothed,
I'd still be programmed to swerve.
I drive these routes with thoughts elsewhere,
assume the worst at every curve.

The lesson here I will proclaim:
Prepare for rough rides day by day,
but still take notice and give thanks
when someone quietly smoothes the way.

Helen Palmer

A Walk in the Park--April

We love our half-mile walk in Patton Park,
paved walkways meandering along a creek,
skirting a man-made pond inhabited by
mallards and Canada geese, with the occasional
sighting of a magisterial heron.

Sally sits and stays on meeting other dogs,
particularly vicious white poodles,
whose mission in life is to cow the larger dogs.
I shake my head at evidence of vandalism,
signs uprooted and thrown into the creek,
water bottles and empty Cheetos bags
abandoned just steps from trash barrels.

The skateboarders and free throwers enjoy
their own precincts, show off their perfect dunks
or death-defying loops on the skate ramp.
We share the boon of a dedicated park.

On this fresh spring day, I wonder where
the female ducks have hidden, sitting on
future ducklings. The clusters of males
hunker down, like men everywhere,
waiting.

And at the side of the path
weeds, blue and lilac creeping charlie,
carpet the bare spots, Nature, as usual,
abhorring a vacuum.   *photo by Helen Palmer*

Helen Palmer

A Walk in the Park--August

It's a shaggy August in the park.
Guarding the roiling creek
(weekly overflowing from deluges of rain)
the weeds stand shoulder high, a mélange
of yellows, blues, greens.

Tired buttercups, Queen Anne's Lace
going to seed, goldenrod just beginning,
the noxious weed with the bell-like blue flower
still creeping along--all speak of excess
of heat and moisture.

The landscape looks unkempt,
as though the gardener
had thrown up his hands
and departed,
leaving everything to autumn's austerity
and winter's frigid winds,
just hoping for
a fresh start in the spring.

Helen Palmer

A Walk in the Park--December

December days, diminished light,
cold winds whip us; we keep our coats closed tight.
Hardy souls walk the circular path
trying to outrun the winter's wrath.

Trees stand stark, branches askew.
The creek runs fast, the pond always low.
Without the blanketing bushes and weeds,
the banks reveal mankind's debris.

Snack wrappers and bottles no one stooped to retrieve
peep from under sticks and sodden leaves.
Miscanthus sinensis lies prone on the bank.
Summer's beauty has fled. We've winter to thank.

Yet the Mallards keep faith. They're still here.
Two domestic white ducks are paddling near.
Dogs and their people greet others with cheer.
We know spring's beauty will enfold us next year.

photo by Helen Palmer

Helen Palmer

Tree City, U. S. A.

We chose our home for its tall trees,
for bushes that would bloom in spring.
We loved our pathways, overgrown,
and branches where the birds could sing.

Now we've grown old and not so spry.
Our treed-in lot can lead to stress.
We spent a day, bundles of cash
on culling out our wilderness.

The maple tree aslant our drive,
its signature shape giving way to rot,
is now reduced to a flat-top trunk,
a surface fit for a flower pot.

Tree surgeons did their forestry
on the 9/11 anniversary.
Our ancient tree was lifted up,
left a gaping hole to the sky.

Helen Palmer

The Dead House

The realtor's tipsy sign
and the paper box
holding only a Christmas
mailbox cover

guard the entrance
to the house next door.
Patches on the asphalt driveway
have not been sealed.

Ivy chokes the dogwood
by the front porch,
twining the trunk
to the top branches.

Unhindered, six-foot tall
weeds have taken over
the side yard, even hiding
the flamboyant Joe Pye.

A carefully-mown patch of grass
beckons to potential purchasers,
asks them to believe in this house,
to bring human life to it again.

Helen Palmer

To See a Prairie

...it takes a clover and one bee...
Here's my bow to Emily.
When I glanced at my neighbor's weeds,
the poet provided me with the seeds

for one more poem. One bee fed
upon one clover. That sight led
me to my quotation store
and the genius of that metaphor.

What hidden boons to our sanity,
the memorization of poetry,
the ability to make us see
the distillation of honey from a bee!

("To make a prairie..." by Emily Dickinson)

Helen Palmer

Legacy

I peer into the mirror
each morning faithfully,
examine upper lip and chin
where chin hairs peek at me.

I hate those pesky outgrowths
that waggle in the breezes,
that cause perfect strangers
to itch to wield a tweezers.

I've never shaped my eyebrows.
My specs get in the way.
But I twist and turn to see my chin
and tweeze those hairs each day.

On my visits to my mother
I viewed her crop with dismay.
My first job was to sit her down
and tweeze those hairs away.

So now I see her image
in the mirror and in a frame.
I remember as I tweeze my chin
from whence those chin hairs came.

(Look Both Ways, 2009)

Helen Palmer

Mountain Laurel

A most unlikely source of beauty
with crooked trunk and gnarled branches,
this evergreen begs to be brushed out
of any forest stand—

until that week in May

when every cluster
shyly, like a debutante,
raises its many flowered face—
each delicate pink bloom a pentagonal
hoopskirt
with ten white stays fanning out
from a pure white waist.

Then the sun, its escort, kisses
these branches
and offers the prize to
anyone
with eyes.

(Jigsaw Puzzle, 1997)

Helen Palmer

Beverly Bryan Russell

Day Lilies

Lilies of the day
we call them.
Others say ditch lilies.

As we drive to Mills River, I tell him,
The roadsides are so beautiful,
I want to jump out,
grab all that
orange-lily glory.

Two days later,
he comes through the kitchen door
with an armload of
the long-stemmed lovelies.

I love them, love him
with his wild flowers,
the anniversary yellow roses each December.
Love him enough for five more decades.

(*Look Both Ways, 2009*)

Trout Lilies

Hiding beneath the forest floor,
trout lilies wait
for March and sunshine sprinkles.
Speckled leaves rise
from that rich decay
along with yellow flowers, bell-like, thin stalks.
Soon over, bloom and leaf disappear
taking this wonder with them
to secret caves beneath our feet.
It takes time to store the strength
for such shy magic.

(Taste of Waking, 2002)

Beverly Bryan Russell

Tomatoes All Year

I want tomatoes all year,
good and juicy,
not cardboard-tasting ones.
By the time January comes,
I say *Give me a tomato,*
don't care what it's like,
just need a tomato.

Pretend it's vine ripe,
pretend it has summer juice,
pretend it comes from the tropics,
sent on secret planes,
below radar.
Rural folk
hear the drone over their roof,
say
What a strange, low sound this time of night.
The pilot must be lost, hope he doesn't crash.

We meet in a hidden field on the Wateree.
In the dark, we break the law.
Men unload the contraband.
We speak Spanish.
I pay cash.
I must feed my habit.
I sell a few to select customers,
but when lunch time comes,
I slather mayo on white bread,
place red slices there.
Settle down, enjoy my summer treat.

(From the Corner of My Eye, 2008)

Beverly Bryan Russell

My Mother's House

Off the freeway
      down the street
      stands the yellow house
      with smells of sweet cooking, tulips blooming,
           and ferns hanging—my safe place.

Fifty years old now
      like the war's end,
      these houses—brown, green, white—
      conceived for the baby boom,
      near this small town,
           near the South's big city.

Families, white and Protestant,
      with fathers who worked,
      and mothers who worked harder,
      nurturing two or three children
           who will grow up and move away.

Decades pass,
      rapid transit devours the town,
      people with tinted skin arrive,
      speaking strange tongues,
           a melting-pot Babel.

New conflicting cultures and poverty,
      spawning crime and gang violence
      as 4 a.m. bullets splinter sleeping houses
      three doors down,
      random violence—no longer random.

Beverly Bryan Russell

Mama dwells on crime,
      magnified by metro media,
      but she won't leave,
      so near family, friends,
      church and bingo hall.

I do know why she stays
      in her house of memories,
      bric-a-brac and curios,
      but I no longer know my safe place,
      the comfort zone rearranged
         with culture shock.

(Standing on Our Words, 1997)

Beverly Bryan Russell

69

Four Acres, Two Houses, One Barn

We were happy when we sold
my husband's home place.
We were going to a better address,
new bathrooms, more bedrooms.
No grass to cut.

Later, we missed so much from the Linda Vista house.
Our arthritic German shepherd craved her warm sun porch.
Our four-year-old wanted small maple trees he could climb,
and his friend, Gloria, next door.
My husband remembered his birth place, family history,
the only home he knew
until his twenties.

I yearned for sunny basement windows,
a great refuge for wintering plants.
I wanted old roses, a winter jasmine bush,
the barn and pasture where we raised a steer,
crown molding in the living room, plum trees,
our vegetable garden,
years of early marriage.

Now the sprawling Four Seasons Boulevard,
with malls, restaurants,
traffic, traffic, traffic,
would be our neighbor.
The "new" house, age thirty-nine,
replaced our nostalgia long ago.
Home is here.

(Look Both Ways, 2009)

Beverly Bryan Russell

70

Picking Up Sticks

Sisyphus had his boulder,
we have our sticks and fallen limbs.
The job never ends.
We pick them up, break them down,
arrange them on the truck,
cover with tarp, tie with rope, and haul
to whatever place will take them,
landfill or neighbor's brush pile.
One by one, we hurl sticks like spears
onto a bigger pile.
Exhausted, at home we admire our stick-free yard
through ibuprofen haze.
It's neat until the next wind, ice,
whatever devil that it is
flings them down to land.
Then we pick up sticks again.

(Telling Questions, 2002)

Beverly Bryan Russell

Two Kaleidoscopes

It was never enough
to gaze into the cardboard tube.
I longed to open it,
grasp the colored patterns,
make them stay in format.
Flowers were like that, too.
I held their scent, their beauty.
At four, I tried to experience
the earth, the grass,
thought I could fly like birds,
follow dogs as they ran from view,
but I loved kaleidoscopes most of all.

On our twenty-fifth wedding anniversary trip
to New Orleans, I discovered
another mysterious beauty,
the city.
I was in ecstasy over
the food, music, fun, trolleys, shops.
In one of them, we saw an exquisite kaleidoscope.
I visited it every day.
Several months later,
I returned home to find a present on my pillow.
Someone special tracked down
an elegant kaleidoscope for me.
I look into it often,
marveling over the colors, patterns.
I see *love.*

(A Long and Winding Road, 2011)

Beverly Bryan Russell

To Cameron

If I could, I would
walk ahead of you
with whisk brooms, red carpets
making your path
smoother, safer.
Once I smoothed your days
with lullabies, hugs.
Now there's only prayer and all of it.
You'll know this truth some day
when your children need red carpets.

(Telling Questions, 2002)

Beverly Bryan Russell

Painting Marsh Island
February 17, 2000

Brush the grasses,
winter-pale and yellow,
shades of sepia, brown, and beige.
Blend green, darken border palms.
Whiten Hugo's twisted trunks.
Add the sky, large and wide,
mostly blue.
Move boats on the channel,
vessels, floating "fool-the-eye" on grass.
Splash in creeks, the big bend pond.
Fill with feathers, put in ducks, egrets,
all who peck and wait
for tides to arrive and to depart.
Add a sunset searing red.

Last, make night and listen,
secret bird calls, noisy mud,
cracking, popping in the dark.

(Taste of Waking, 2000)

Beverly Bryan Russell

Lost

All morning, the poem follows me everywhere,
bank, pharmacy, library, grocery store.
Suffers mild irritation at the teller,
just a quick drive-up, *have a good day.*
Whines wistfully at the drug store.
Smiles in the library,
(books bring comfort).
Drums its fingers on a cookie box,
presses its head to cold wine bottles in the grocery basket.
Throws a fit
and runs off down the highway
by the produce stand.
Beats me home, sulks.
Later, we sit down together.
It speaks in stilted prose,
seldom smiles,
vanishes into cyberspace.
Lost.

(From the Corner of My Eye, 2008)

Beverly Bryan Russell

Three Days to Saint Simons Island

We didn't look the same.
The last three years had added to the aging process.
Before I arrived, I worried that my legs
would present the most purple veins.
Actually, I had fewer.
Sarah had more wrinkles.
Connie, a big tummy.
Becky had frizzy hair.
My posture was the worst.
We also brought to the weekend
our problems,
two divorces, children, grandchildren, illness,
bitterness toward a late ex-husband.
We relived funny events from fifty years,
took a polite stab at politics.
We dined out, sunned on the beach
wearing hats that made us look like old ladies.
It was wonderful to see these people I love
and who love me.
Then back to the freeways toward home.

Beverly Bryan Russell

A Doraville Memoir

Happy Birthday to Susie, dear friend, best friend
October, 1999

In Doraville, Georgia, our summers were ripe with possibilities.
      Peachtree Road, hot and humid,
        without television, computers, air conditioning.
We had, instead, treasured days of nothing to do,
      but we were never bored.

Our world revolved with childish delights,
      the Club House, a weathered shed sitting under
      the pines in your backyard.
We displayed our nature collections there,
      bird feathers, nests, and captured creatures
      from the pond and creek,
      crawfish, tadpoles, turtles, ending their days
      in the miserable captivity of old mayonnaise jars,
      a similar fate, too, for fireflies
      caught on early June nights.
We also attended to our special duty, making the world
      safe from wasps.
We pelted their nest with stones; they pelted us
      with fierce wasp wrath.

At the drugstore, a nickel or two would buy a cherry Coke,
      carbonated with a swish, and frosted ice cream floats.
We loved reaching into the icy drink box at McElroy's
      pulling up sodas like dripping fish whose water
      fell on our bare, tough summer feet.

Camping out in the back yard, making endless trips to the
      house for supplies, the night you met a snake
      on that ivy-trimmed path.
You recovered well, thanks to your daddy's fast drive
      to the Chamblee Clinic.
It made a good story to tell when school began
      after Labor Day.

Beverly Bryan Russell

Books were our quiet time,
> Nancy Drew, *Anne of Green Gables,*
> Louisa Alcott, and before we were twelve,
> *Gone with the Wind*, which we considered
> non-fiction.
At Sunday school, we gave freely, righteously
> to the iron man piggy bank
> just to see him nod his head and wave.
We memorized our catechism, learned the books
> of the Bible, devout as saints we were,
> yet still lapsed into stifled giggling fits
> during Sunday sermons.

Grammar school days were endless, yet painless.
> We learned to read with Mrs. White,
> to write cursively with Mrs. Gunter,
> to take names for Miss Taylor (she loved
> the teachers' lounge), to multiply
> with Mrs. Price, to make *papier-mache*
> pilgrims with Mrs. Cowan,
> to worry about the Cold War with Mrs. Bickers,
> and to do great projects with Mrs. Fryer.

Our secondary years were different.
> We were small fish in Chamblee High's
> big pond. Algebra was my nemesis. You
> always buckled down and got it.
> Facing adolescent worries about boys
> and body image, we had brief crushes
> on guys who briefly loved us back.
> The sophomore hunk fell in love with you,
> to our great envy and awe.
> We both had serious beaus, but
> luck was with us, they didn't last.

After high school, we left Doraville and neither of us
> lived there for very long again.

Beverly Bryan Russell

We share so much history.
You were a bridesmaid at my wedding.
My little brother, Jimmy, disgracefully decorated
        Stewart's car before your honeymoon escape.

We are different.
You are a genetic Republican.
My family, always Democrats,
yet we still discuss politics.
You live in a planned community.
I live in a community that plans to destroy itself
        with zoneless development.

We are alike, too.
We each have one perfect child,
        Saint Allison and Saint Cameron.
We each have one perfect husband.
We each love antiquing, poring over good buys,
        expensive trifles.
And we can still pick up the conversation we began
        two months or twenty years ago.

When people ask if I have siblings, I say *three*.
        One brother, two sisters, my biological one
        and my soul sister, Susie.

Susie and Beverly   family photo

(Telling Questions, 2002)

Beverly Bryan Russell

School year, 1945-46, Doraville, Ga.

At the end of summer our aunts told us goodbye and said,
Beverly, the next time we see you, you will know how to read.
I thought, *That will be very hard.*
However, I soon slipped into that delight of all joys.

My teacher, Laura White, was a bit gruff.
Mama said it was because she lost her husband in a lake.
I wondered why they didn't just go look for him.

School was great, except we had to Behave.
My first report was strange.
I made all A's, but I was marked rude, discourteous.
Mama said, *You need to Behave and be nicer to everyone.*

Mornings, my Daddy drove me to school.
I was so embarrassed every day.
World War Two had just ended.
For us, the Model A of long vintage was all we had.
Daddy had to crank it by hand.
The older boys stood outside and laughed.

The biggest, most wonderful happiness
was making friends with Martha Sue Bracewell, Susie.
When Susie had scarlet fever, I wanted to get it, too.

Toward spring I began to hear about Passing.
If you didn't Pass, you had to read about
Jane and Bob with their dumb pets another time.

I had discovered more interesting books.
And I had been rude and discourteous.
I was really happy when I found that did not matter.

Beverly Bryan Russell

80

The Family Wash Pot (1900-2009)

It is older than I am.
If this Wash Pot could talk
I would hear about
the woman whose name was Early,
who was married to Noble
who worked for my father's family.
Early washed the clothes,
cleaned the house, did some of the cooking.
Noble worked the farm.

Each wash day hot soapy suds and Early produced
clean cotton clothes.
At Thanksgiving some relatives killed hogs.
The Wash Pot knew many butchered swine.

Now, time has deemed the Wash Pot an antique,
a greenish iron receptacle
where I plant ornamental kale,
pansies in fall,
begonias in summer.
Standing at the kitchen window,
I see this container often,
think

Early, Noble, aunts, uncles, father.

Beverly Bryan Russell

Karen Heggen

Understory

In these southern mountains, November
begins the season of the long view.

This year nature's timetable has been skewed
by the weight of heavy rains on summer's watch
which held back the impetus of potential energy
normally built up in spring.

The mantle of leaves which cloaked the curves
of the ridges has flaked away, leaving the dermis
of limbs to wrestle with the winter winds.

Thus begins the long season when lambent light
reaches the understory.

The Long View

First days of spring
had us bundled against
icy winds and chilly rains
unsurpassed in winter.

We welcome the advancing
buds, worry for their survival.
We entertain weeks of joy
as flashes of feathers catch our eye,
and bird song floods our ears,
as seed caps swell, as branches
blush, as sweet scents serenade
our nostrils, before pollen covers
our cars, causes sneezing and
swelling, a price to pay for
the promise of spring.

This year, I wish I could freeze-frame
one gift of late winter, *the long view*,
for it seems the advancing leaves
too soon obscure the outlines of trees,
the evidence of houses and barns
along roadways and among neighbors.

Perhaps it is my own aging pace
that yearns to hold the snapshot
of infant spring, rather than run pell-mell
through the dance of exuberant youth,
the heady scent of passion, the urgent
onslaught of full-blown green
that obscures the long-treasured
long view.

Karen Heggen

Puzzle

If it were winter would I worry more?
And how should I describe it,
purr or *snore*?

As I lie here upon the couch
that noise I hear, is it *inside*
or is it *outside* my house?

The window is just above my head,
and yet no cat sits on the sill as I stir,
late night, from my late summer bed.

Is there a space where doves might nest?
If so, is night a time they coo?
Or do they rest?

I've seen opossums on their evening strolls,
but midnight snoring?
Is *that* among their goals?

This sound I hear is one that comes and goes.
Some nights I've thought
it might be *my own nose*.

Yet when I finally held my breath, on it went.
Wore me down,
left me spent.

Only silence now, so I'll put down my pen
and close my eyes
and try to sleep *again*.

Do Goats Smile?

Remember when
you caught a glimpse
out of the corner of your eye
of something that had been
there all along on your path
but gone unnoticed.

Last week, a mile and a half from home
on the two-lane back from town,
I turned my head in time to catch sight
of a small white goat, with long hair,
perched atop the metal roof of his house.

I swear he smiled with satisfaction
at the warm spring day, the play his
goat feet had made on the tin roof,
the comfort of his tiny valley, tucked
between two hills, not two blocks
from the Baptist church, the drivers'
license station, the bowling alley.

He had turned his back on the traffic,
his head turned ever so slightly sideways,
so that smile of satisfaction showed.

Karen Heggen

How Long Will There Be Horses?

New hope this week, as I count two more
unseen before, not a mile from my door,
along *US 25*, heading toward town.

Brown one was, the other black,
half-hidden by grass, but backed
by a half-century-old red brick ranch.

I celebrate each chance that
their numbers not diminish,
in our county, in our country.

Horses are my romance,
not some daily dance I make
of hauling feed, mucking stalls.

Horses' large eyes affirm my calls
of praise, yet should I raise a cry,
their tails twitch as if to swat a fly.

Drought and increased cost
of human needs in recent years
caused beloved horses to be sold.

Just last winter, one I know was sold outright,
Star, black, the son of *Patches* and *Shadow*.
His burro buddy, *Jack*, went to a friend.

That crew I knew as the *Boon Companions*.
They lived on a curve of Berkley Road,
across from a factory, a mile from the mall.

I give thanks for all the horses
I still can view a mile or two from town.
May space for them live on.

Karen Heggen

87

Bold Blue Aster

I have loved the stately,
long-blooming Aster Tataricus
for more than twenty years.
Long ago I wrote a poem about it.

Its great blue heads have graced
an edge of lawn since the original,
now nine years gone
to highway construction,
greeted guests along the two-lane.

Fine Gardening reminds me
that this aster blooms for
a longer season than any other.
Low maintenance, no staking required.
You can look it in the eye.

Today Wikipedia adds two new
grace notes to increase my love.

Aster Tataricus is one of the fifty
fundamental herbs of Chinese Medicine.
Its antibacterial action inhibits the growth
of many nasty and prevalent bacteria.

In Japan it is called *shion* which in the language
of flowers translates to *I won't forget you.*

Karen Heggen

She Nods to Autumn

She holds her head high.
Her crown, transformed
to translucent wisps,
is fragile as fish bones,
a ghostly echo of its
recent and distant splendor.

Her dress is fading.
It droops around the edges.
She bends to the winds
of change, yet rises
resilient and graceful.

Her seed has flown.
Her posture remains
proud at the passing.
She stands along
the roadside, where
she waved at other
seasons' changes.

One fine brushstroke
of brittleness begins
to show, forecast
of fire and snow
sketched
in the coming scene.

Shine on,
mid-autumn grass,
Miscanthus sinensis.

Karen Heggen

Aunt Thora, Two Photos

Born before the telephone.
Born before electric lights.
Born in Norway, 1879.
She came to Wisconsin, 1901.
Worked as ship's cook to pay passage.
See the Gibson Girl upsweep
of her long red hair that year.
It grew longer yet.
It sweeps the ground
in the photo, 1933.
She wore it in a braid atop her head.
Brushed it every night.
Washed it only twice a year.
Kept it clean by brushing
cornmeal through it.
Her color faded, but never grayed.
At eighty she cut it to her waist.
Eased the weight of her braid.
Thora Saxhaug who never married
took care of me when I was born.
I always knew the braid.
Knew her as *Aunt* Thora
(what my father called her.)
I never knew the sight of
that floor-length hair except
in my imagination until
some forty years after she died.
My sister sent the photos she had gained
from the History Museum Director
in Ashland, Wisconsin—a descendant
of one of Thora's sisters.

family photos

Karen Heggen

90

Wash and Wear

The young today may be unaware
how lives have changed since wash and wear.

Wash and wear came with nylon and polyester.
Today's cotton blends make fabric feel softer.

The clothes dryer is an appliance we wanted
and one we have come to take for granted.

Today dryer sheets prevent *static cling,*
but let us remember there was no such thing

when cotton and linen were what we wore--
washed and hung on a line outside before
we brought them inside to starch and iron.

What a blessing it was when the steam iron came.
Wrinkles in clothes became easy to tame.
You rarely see a clothes line or the steam iron today.

Wash and wear we now call permanent press.
We are simpler now in the way we dress.
We reach for the steam iron less and less.

Still, everything old is new again.
You'll find lots of easy-wrinkle rayon
among the labels on today's fashions.

Karen Heggen

While Searching the Past

While searching the past today
      I found a black sheep, Adam Sprackling,
      Englishman, who stabbed his wife in 1652
      and was hanged for it in 1653.

While searching the past in 1991
      I found a card with the name Betty Camin
      in a note I had made at a nearby library in 1988.
      It was from a wooden box of surnames from 1976.

While searching the past today
      I found Betty Camin, and remembered her
      as a professional genealogist who shares
      my mother's maiden name: Spradling.

While searching for Betty Camin in 1991
      I called information in Raleigh NC and found
      two Camins. Called one who proved to be her son.
      He said she had moved to Mt. Airy, gave me her number.

When I contacted Betty Camin in 1991
      she invited me to visit her. I did. She told me of a client
      for whom a black sheep turned up among many white-bread
      ancestors. She had wondered whether to tell her.

When Betty Camin contacted her client and told her
      about the black sheep, the client told Betty
      Drop everything else and follow the black sheep.

While the black sheep I found again today may or may not
      be related to my mother's ancient paternal line,
      his notoriety had kept him in the local annals of Thanet
      and was why he had to be buried without St. Lawrence
      Church, though his wife and forebears are buried within.

Karen Heggen

Meditation upon a Youth Long Gone

*(After reading Tichborne's Elegy from 1586 *)*

Now here, by age beset, remain some glories yet.
Now what was young is old, unstrung, a broken chain.
Now though life's hum has come undone, the story yet
remains, and from the ruins rakes a token gain--
a hoard of molten memories is freely shared.
Taste *then* whose open maw it is that now is bared.

Some still in age the story tell of old, of youth reborn.
Some well remembered images, still green, ring bold.
Some threads of gold, the tattered garment still adorn,
whose layers lend a warmth against the winter's cold,
and blood of ages reddens what was once impaired.
Then, pulses bloom and ecstasy in age is dared.

Though, Death, your options you hold dear, *look*, I'm still here,
to peel the brittle husk away, and dance and sing,
if only in my mind each day. Some say *it's queer.*
I say, you're welcome to your dreary ways. You bring
but proof that yet your plaintive suffering I've been spared.
My soul will sing as life's last trumpet note is heard.

Tichborne was executed in his twenties for a plot to murder
Queen Elizabeth I, an attempt to restore Catholicism through
Mary, Queen of Scotts. See Tichborne's Elegy here:
http://en.wikipedia.org/wiki/Chidiock Tichborne
My elegy above imagines passion such as his at a greater age.

Karen Heggen

Available Light

Familiar term for photos without flash, it came to her after
she was steeped in art books, habitual late-winter reading
to refresh her memory of how colors can appear so different
in familiar things at different times of day, amended in each season.

The moon would be full, the eastern hills were already indigo
dotted with fireflies she knew to be not only the warm glow
from home windows, but *safety lights*, an oxymoron of sorts,
since they were what gave the night horizon an orange glaze,
made the earth glow at night for airline pilots and passengers,
for cameras in space...

As though groundlings held *dark* the greatest danger, while lulled
by artificial light, the bright glow of TV and computer screens
which clothe dark predictions and dramatic situations in the light
of bright solicitations, showing how we can pop a pill, sign up for
a cell phone, sandwich and fries, satellite dish, Sport Utility Vehicle,
and carve out our place in the bright lights, *keep the dark at bay*.

What they *don't say*, is that our deepest roots grow in darkness.
Contrasts are what shape our *vision*.
Low level light opens us to *mystery*, the *Other*, the unexplained,
which haunted childhood's history.

Now adults, let us call *our own* the embrace of the unknown,
in reverence hold the dual gifts of light and dark, the rhythms
of Life's dance, reread the old hymns, the ancient scriptures
without the strictures we saw with child's eyes.
May we with age grow *wise*, learn to *treasure*
the gifts given by *contrasts*.

Karen Heggen

Love Among the Ruins

1

Today's news carried a story that resurrected
the truth of the only Sunday sermon
I still remember from my childhood.

NPR and then AP celebrated the successful mating
of two Canada Geese, whose handicaps would seem
to some to have doomed them to lives of hellish limitation.

The goose, Miss Canada, has no lower bill.
Without it, she can't eat as other geese do.
So, she found another way to feed.

At an animal rehabilitation shelter she learned
to flip her food up the side of the bowl, gulp it down,
and finish with a water wash-down.

Still, without a bill, she can't preen herself,
an act essential to geese, to spread oil to their feathers,
keeping the body warm, dry, and afloat.

Take a gander, Toronto, whose mangled right wing
required amputation. He will never again fly with the flock.
Put these two together, and you get a little bit of heaven.

You see, *he* preens *her. She* stands by *him,*
and could create quite a flap if she needed to protect him.
Their ministrations have led to mating.

It is the pattern of geese to mate for life.
Though no goslings were reported, the procreative
power of this pair is already bearing witness.

Karen Heggen

2

Across the years, I see the minister in the pulpit
plump up his feathers, raise his head,
and honk out a homily that reverberates
in my bones right now, six decades from that day.

It is the tale of two men visiting Hell,
(Dante and Virgil I later learned.) The visitor
is surprised to see a long banquet table loaded
with copious quantities of the finest food and drink.

Before his mind can fathom why Hell should be
so well provisioned, his ears are assaulted
by shrieking and cursing, compounded by sounds
of crashing dishes plus pounding on floor and furniture.

He sees that each person at the table has only one hand
free to feed himself. For each one, the other hand
is tied behind his back. The din grows louder.
The visitor, overwhelmed, asks to be shown to Heaven.

As they approach Heaven, the visitor is heartened
by the sound of laughter and music. Once inside, he is
startled to see a long banquet table, filled with fine food,
and each guest with one hand tied behind his back.

He turns to his guide in astonishment.
There is no favor in Heaven, he cries.
They are the same!

"Ah, look again," his guide reassures.
"Heaven is indeed favored,
for *here beings feed one another,*
while in Hell they only feed themselves."

Karen Heggen

Yolanda

A musical sound.
A beautiful name.
A mysterious word
at the edge of waking.

A beautiful flower,
Violet, I learn ,
a royal name
of long ago.

Gratitude awakens
a picture in mind…
Yolanda, queenly tall,
ebony black, lilting voice,
winning smile, gentle hands,
mothering ways *to me*,
old enough to be *her* mother.
Yolanda from the nursing facility
that housed me twice in two years.

Yolanda, mother of a near-grown daughter.
Her name reminded me of the equally musical
Cecelia,
a song of my youth by Simon and Garfunkel,
Yolanda did not know it.

Today I learn that Yolanda was the name
given by Martin Luther King, Jr. and
Coretta Scott King to their eldest daughter.

Yolanda is also a name in recent songs,
songs *I have never heard*.
I hope they are beautiful.

Karen Heggen

A Bed Poem

Long ago we heard it said *we spend a third of life in bed.*
Though a lesser fraction may stand instead,
let us consider of our lives in bed…

How long in life was your bed your own?
Which side of one *shared* did you call your own?
Did a book keep you company?
Or, perhaps, it was music or late night TV.
Did a child or a pet break your reverie?

What was the mattress, what the frame?
Of heat or of cold did you complain?
What the bed's place against a wall?
Did you sleep far or near to the bathroom hall?

What the table, what the lamp
added to comfort or feeling cramped?
What were the sounds at night you heard?
(Sibling, spouse, perhaps a bird?)

Some sleep high, some sleep low,
bolsters behind or pillows below.
On your side or on your back?
(Tummy sleeping can cause a lack.)

And when you slept away from home
at relatives, friends, together/alone
at condo, cruise ship, hostel or hotel,
do you remember, did you sleep well?

In conversation a game to wage
is where we've slept from age to age.
Or write down your history on the page,
your beds and bedrooms from stage to stage.

Karen Heggen

98

Lost and Found

It's not the things we have,
but the memories we make of them.
So says the announcer's voice
each week on Antiques Roadshow.

Confirmation came again today
with the news that a college class ring,
missing for sixty years, was found
in a dried-out lake bed in West Texas
and will be returned to its owner
who now lives in Washington state--
eighty-four-year-old Addie Elizabeth Little Clark.

The ring will be presented
at a family reunion in Texas
by the woman who found it.

I *worked hard to earn it,*
recalled the relieved owner,
the only one of sixteen siblings
who was able to attend college.

She and her husband-to-be were wading in the lake
the year after graduation and had not known
where the ring went missing.

It was the initials AEL engraved inside the ring
that allowed the Alumni Association to identify the owner
after a member drove forty miles to retrieve it from the finder.

Old memories rise and new ones take shape
in these acts of generosity and celebration.

Karen Heggen *photo by Karen Heggen*

The Seasoned Poets of the Blue Ridge
Anthologies: 1994 - 2014

Elda Lepak

Just as It Did

Just as it did when I was one
the sun does rise and set
and rivers flow and
trees bear fruit
and babies tend to cry.

Just as it did when I was thirty
the moon and the stars still shine
and lovers love and
they bear fruit
and babies tend to cry.

Just as it did when I was sixty
the rain and snow still fall
and seasons pass and
years add up
and babies tend to cry.

(*Sky Canvas*, 2010)

The Sound of Silence

I like the sound of silence at night
when even the birds sleep
and darkness surrounds me.
Outside, the stars find rest
behind scattered clouds
leaving only the dim moon
to serve as my night light.
I wander the quiet house
in search of an afghan to cuddle under.
Sitting in that peaceful place
with paper and a pencil in hand
I write out the words
that sift through silent thoughts.
Reflections bubble up,
sometimes boil down to an idea.
I may conjure up a wish list, a to-do list,
or decide to paint the guest room green.
But sometimes I get a poem,
like this one.

Elda Lepak

Moonglow

Eight to fifteen feet above us,
twelve tethered hot air balloons
float in the late evening sky.
We sit in chairs
or sprawl out on blankets
to watch the balloons bob
and shift in the breeze.
A rush of hot air pushed by flames
creates a roar and a burst of light.
Balloons flash and dim
looking like well dressed fireflies
dancing in the dark.

I remember the fields
we ran through long ago
sweeping minnow nets
or mason jars across the darkness,
capturing the flashes of white
that became our night lights.
Even then we would ooooh
and ahhh at the moonglow.

Elda Lepak

My Sister's Friend

Her real name was Victoria.
I remember she was adorable
and often dressed in pink.
The clothes she wore were
carefully cut out and fitted,
hand made with love.
She had a bed of her own
with tiny flowers on its cover.

She was talked to, read to,
sung to, toted along everywhere.
She traveled with our family
and was a welcomed playmate.
Like many childhood friends
she was lost along the way.

I remember her big eyes,
her pink nose and long ears.
Vicki, as we called her,
was a three-inch paper rabbit,
a paper friend who slept in
a paper match box
with a cotton ball for her pillow.

Elda Lepak

The Cat in the Manger

It must have been something
about the olive wood that attracted
the cat to the manger scene.
How carefully she stepped
through the camels and sheep,
knocking over only one wise man
and a shepherd boy.

Her goal was baby Jesus,
asleep in the manger.
How she managed to lift Him out
and jump to the floor
I am not certain.
Every few days poor baby Jesus
was found on the carpet,
wet and abandoned.

Then, Jesus disappeared.
We found a small plastic replacement
that the cat never disturbed.

When moving, we found Jesus
as men shifted the bookcase.
Either Jesus was batted under it,
or in frustration of being so poorly treated,
He crawled to safety.
The movers were not certain
of what was happening as I shouted
Baby Jesus!!
Born again, Jesus lies in the manger.

Elda Lepak

105

Breakfast Is Served

The unfamiliar sound of quiet
drew me into the living room
from making beds down the hall.
I was greeted with the sweet smell
of chocolate frosting and the sight
of cup cakes slathered
on my children's hands and faces,
embedded in the sofa,
in the fur of the happy dog.

It was just a reminder not to leave cupcakes
on the counter when the three-year-old
had learned to push, to climb a chair.
He evidently had also learned to share
and passed cupcakes all around.
They didn't even blink
when they saw me coming.
They smiled, she in droopy diapers,
he in Big Bird pajamas,
dog in sticky fur.

I joined them with a cupcake.
In what order should I clean them—
dog, kids, sofa?
I was upset enough to forget
to take a picture, but could hardly
fault the kid for using new found skills.
The dog was just an opportunist.

(Song of the San Joaquin, 2014)
(Honorable Mention, Humorous Poem, California Federation
of Chapparral Poets, Inc. 2014)

Elda Lepak

Eingo and Pym

My son had two imaginary playmates
that played trucks and tag with him.
Once he warned me
I was about to sit on Pym at the dinner table.
Alan's friends did not surprise or concern me.
I did wonder where he got their names.

My grandfather was a shaman
in Finland, known for his talk of spirits,
his use of healing herbs and spells.
He came to the U.S. in 1895,
where his skills were not appreciated,
his position as shaman not recognized.
My family history includes ghosts
and strange events, and stories abound.

Alan stopped talking to Eingo and Pym
when we moved from Pennsylvania.
A few years later I was going through
some story books in his school room.
There was a battered book about
colonial times in Pennsylvania.
It was about a family, with children.
Two of the children
were Eingo and Pym.

Elda Lepak

A Visit from Sandy

Last night our long-departed dog, Sandy,
and I were riding bikes along a narrow road.
That is, I was riding, she was running
with ears flapping, scruffy fur flying.

We stopped at a simple, unfamiliar,
long, old cafe where I parked my bike
along a cream cement wall. We both entered
as if we had done this many times.

I walked around the counter, down a row of booths,
and to a four-top table where I sat and spoke
with two friends. I assumed they were friends
even though I have no idea who they were.

I had a cold, foamy beer and French fries.
Sandy, sitting on her back haunches
with front paws waving, sneezed
in sets of three–her request for a share.

I don't remember the conversation
but remember eating, saying good-bye,
and walking out of the cafe
with Sandy bouncing after me.

On the way home we encountered a German shepherd.
I didn't recognize him, but I knew the routine.
Sandy ran up to him growling, ready for a fight.
I thought, *Heavens, nothing has changed.*

The Napoleon complex lived on,
Sandy, the cockapoo, still had not learned.
Luckily, the German shepherd knew his kind
and walked off. Unimpressed.

Elda Lepak

Spirits in the Sky

The moon is low, large, and the color
of melted yellow and orange crayons.
Gentle winds pull and stretch
wispy clouds across the dark sky,
back lit by the candlelight of the moon.
An eerie face with raised eye brows
above close deep-set eyes appears.
A bulbous nose almost hides a quiet mouth
poised to say something.

Minutes later, an impish face with laughing eyes
peers down from within the thick branches
of a summer green tree.
A sudden breeze rearranges the leaves
and the face vanishes.

I like to think they are spirits
playing, wandering,
caught for an instant by a mere mortal.

Elda Lepak

Someday Gray

someday is a gray word
neither inviting or exciting
vague, it promises little

hard to hear when young
as I knew *someday*
was a long way off

hard to say when older
as I knew *someday*
was an untenable dream

hard to face when old
as I know my *someday*,
my end day, is coming fast

yet I would rather think
in *someday* gray
as *never* is forever black

(Free Verse, Issue 99/100, 2009)

Elda Lepak

Cardinal Envy

The female cardinal
is not blessed
to wear the brilliant color
of her flashy mate.
Both are noisy.
Perhaps they argue.
She, jealous of his red,
his ability to catch attention
wherever he perches.

In frustration she preens,
seeks confirmation of her beauty.
She is resourceful,
discovers side view mirrors
and windows Windex-clean.
She looks, then rages,
slams into each reflective surface.
Like a daily fix
she returns and repeats—
result—
blunt force suicide.

Elda Lepak

Summer Storm Sequence

A crescendo of thunder
rolls along with graying clouds
playing bumper-pool across the sky.
Lightning, like fractured arrows, flashes
towards earth, lands with deafening snaps.
Rain follows as if someone unzipped the heavens.
Wind chases the deluge sideways
until it hits the house with the force of a pressure hose.
The skies relax, tired after their dramatic display.
Clouds drop a steady patter of rain,
empty their last load.

The grass shivers in relief, stretches tall.
Flowers raise their faces, shake off the muddy dust,
and sponge up the needed moisture.
Birds emerge from their tree branch shelters,
swoop through the lingering drops.
They sing, anticipate the feast of surfacing worms.

The sun finds a hole and punches through,
making rooftops glisten.
Trees dazzle with iridescent glitter.
The cooling air smells fresh, like line-dried sheets.
One last soft rumble of thunder rolls off
the distant drifting clouds.

(*Seasoned Poetry*, 2013)

Elda Lepak

Driving Rural Roads

Aging barns still stand
with warped gray boards
and tired drooping doors.
But for the stone fireplaces
the houses are gone.

Neglected orchards eke
out a few blossoms each spring,
and offer fewer apples each fall.
All signs of gardens are gone.

Mossy rails on split wood fences
lean in, hug one another for support.
Weeds and wild flowers choke the fields.
The animals and machinery are gone.

The land continues to rest as it waits
for people to return.

(First Place SilverArts Competition,
Henderson County, NC, 2014)

Elda Lepak

Blue Grass Music Friday Night

Banjos, guitars, and fiddles
sway to their own lively music
in the arms of five old men
wearing faded shirts, tired jeans,
and dusty boots.
One man must be ninety-five,
his skin as gray as his tousled hair,
his eyes a quiet blue.
No expression on his face,
he just plays on, mechanically,
as he has done for years.
Between numbers, he rubs his hands,
flexes his fingers, urges them on.

Young vocalists sing the area's history,
all enthusiastic, some off key.
The forgiving audience joins in,
the old man mouths the words.
The set closes with applause.
The old man shuffles across the stage,
grabs the railing as he descends the steps.
A young girl with brown curly hair,
a short flared skirt, and brand new boots
grins at the old man, raises her fiddle.
She turns to wave her bow to friends
and races to join the group on stage.
The old man smiles–that smile of satisfaction.
Tradition, transition. It's all good.

Elda Lepak

114

Life's Knots

The knots I couldn't unsnaggle
began with knots in my hair and
progressed to knots in my shoelaces.

Knots tangled in my stomach
when I became lost on my way home
from kindergarten.
And when I had to memorize anything,
face any difficult test,
or had to speak before a class.

There were hard knots of kids
on the playground and
loose knots of people at work.
I had a corded knot puzzle,
and landed in some love knots.
My crocheting resembles a
scramble of knots.

I learned to untie them,
untangle them,
face them, get over them,
live with them,
but some of them I have not.

(Song of the San Joaquin, 2014)

Elda Lepak

Pay Attention to the Pretty

It is so easy to ignore.
We dwell only within our thoughts,
never taking time to observe
wonders that surround us each day.

The color of the sky above—
it is so easy to ignore,
like flowers of every spring
going unnoticed as they bloom.

The flight of a bird is magic,
yet, as it glides and swoops with grace,
it is so easy to ignore.
Pay attention to the pretty.

Return smiles on passing faces.
Touch the statue on the corner.
Life is changing, time is passing.
It is so easy to ignore.

Elda Lepak

A Red Leaf Falls

A red tipped leaf lies upon my path.
It seems early for leaves to fall.

I watch flowers fade, their petals curl,
losing stamina as evenings cool.

My birthdays come and go and I feel
no different from one day to the next.

It is autumn that repeats a pattern of aging,
reminding me I am failing, falling apart.

It is then my bones grow cold, I note more gray,
have aches that delay my morning meandering.

The skies are dark and brisk winds whisk away
remaining colors from now stark trees.

I follow the trees and flowers into autumn
and age again when a red leaf falls.

(Look Both Ways, 2009)　　**Elda Lepak**

Memories through Our Changing Seasons

The Seasoned Poets of the Blue Ridge

20 years: 1994 - 2014

*Laurabeth "Rusty" Breeding
Connie Elder
*Hazel Fryer *d*
*Karen Heggen
Elda Lepak
Betty Martinez
*Gwyneth Noble
*Helen Palmer
*Edith Pedersen *d*
Beverly Russell
Frances Schneider *d*
*Helen van Boer

Key
   Charter Member: 1994 *
   Deceased *d*

December 1998. At the Henderson Country Library
Hazel Fryer, Frances Schneider, Helen van Boer,* Karen Heggen,* "Rusty"*
Breeding, Betty Martinez, Helen Palmer,* Edith Pederson, and *Gwyneth Noble.*

Tribute to Poets

Frances Miner Schneider
(1904 - 2003)

Haying Time

I remember haying time
whenever I smell fresh-cut grass.
The noise of the mowing machine
as the horses pulled it
through the field,
how the fast-moving blades shuddered
through the clover and the tall timothy
felling them for winter feed.
I remember riding over
a bumble bee's nest
and the sting that gave me
a lump over one eye.

The horses pranced in pain and terror.
My father rushed from the near-by wagon
to hold and calm the horses
to keep them from running away
with me and the machine.
We were lathered and quivering,
the horses and I.
My father looked at the sun.
"It's time to quit
for today," he said.
"We'll finish cutting the field tomorrow."

(Haying Time, 1997)

Legacy
to my daughter

I've thought of many things
that I might want to leave you
when I'm gone.
Shall it be a memory
or something you can touch?
> The many days
> we took our picnics to the park.
> We walked the paths
> found a host of treasures
> as we walked.
> Silver spider webs in bushes
> wooly worms black and brown
> crawling off to make cocoons
> for winter.

You always loved
the stories of grandparents
coming to America from Europe.
Of how five brothers and a father
came to Michigan
where the lumber was abundant.
> In a factory family-built
> they plied their trade
> as cabinet makers,
> learned earlier in Germany.

This table with its filigree carvings
and its marble top
fashioned by my great-grandfather
as a gift for his bride
on their wedding day.
> Its worth in worldly goods is little.
> It is part of our early family.
> You and I treasure it.
> You will tell the story to your children.
> They will understand our love
> of Grandma's table with its marble top.

(Swimming in Stars, 1998)

Frances Miner Schneider

121

Hazel Herdon Fryer
(1914 - 2003)

Ronald

Sometimes I sit on the bench
with Ronald
at McDonald's
in Wal-Mart.
>I like his optimistic colors,
>bright yellow and orange,
>settle down to watch
>"the passing parade."

Young couples holding hands
hurrying along
thinking only
of themselves.
>Mommies seriously shopping,
>baby in cart, two youngsters trailing.
>Daddies taking Saturday duty
>struggling to learn nurturing.

Grandpas and Grandmas
making their way to the pharmacy,
feet clad in clumsy
but comfortable shoes.
>People of all shapes,
>sizes, fashions, passing by smiling.
>"Does he talk to you?"
>one man asks.

"You' better watch that guy!"
says another.
Children hop up,
sit on Ronald's lap.
>With his arm across
>my shoulders
>my grin matching his,
>like Ronald, I feel so beloved
>by everyone!

(Standing on Our Words, 1997)

Once Upon a Time

As I was dressing my son
for first kindergarten
my elderly father said,
You're turning him over
to the world now.

Today that echo rings in my
ears as my
great-grandson
smiles up at me,
a great-grandmother

lost in a puzzling new world
of computer viruses
credit card misuse
school shootings
child abuse.

I hug our little boy, look
into his innocent eyes
but never without
the white flag
of Hope
the true flag
of Prayer.

(Paper Trail, 2001)

Hazel Herdon Fryer

123

Edith Pederson
(1922 - 2008)

Instant Recall

Part of my past returned to me today.
A carton too big to fit the box was left
on my doorstep by the postman.
Addressed from my cousin, it presented
a mystery. Jeanne and I are infrequent correspondents
and rarely send packages.

In great puzzlement I opened it to find
a long evening cape of burgundy velvet
lined with white satin. As I draped it
over my shoulders, scenes of years past
came rushing back—Junior-Senior dance,
Senior Banquet, girls in long dresses,
boys in best suits and slicked-down hair
dancing cheek to cheek.

Especially vivid was my first grown-up visit
to a Boston Pops concert. Sitting at a little round
table with Mother, sipping a "Shirley Temple" highball,
wearing a full-skirted, off-the-shoulder white gown,
I pretended to be unconcerned but was secretly reveling
in admiring glances from nearby listeners.

Not long after that my civilian clothes were packed away,
to be exchanged for the Navy blue uniform of a W.A.V.E.
The dress later became the basis of my wedding gown.
The cape disappeared in fact, and in memory,
probably passing from one cousin to another
before being tucked back in someone's closet,
only to reappear more than fifty years later.

(Swimming in Stars, 1998)

The Five and Dime

I mourn the passing of the 5 & 10 cent store
with its wooden counters that held
so many marvelous things.
A child could wander,
dimes and pennies clutched in hand
or clinking in small change purse,
looking for just the right bottle of perfume
for Mother, pencil and pad for school.

Each counter was divided into bins of varied sizes
and held many wonderful, unwrapped items,
with no stiff, sterile wrappings of tear-resistant
plastic to get in the way.
A shopper could turn, touch,
examine with careful fingers
under the stern eyes of salesladies who paced
quietly along the aisles.
We always wondered how they could move
so silently on those wooden floorboards.

The lunch counter, along one wall, had stools
that swiveled all the way around
and usually squeaked out of tune. They sold
an amazing array of food, from coffee and doughnuts
to a blue plate special of meat, potatoes and
two vegetables.

(The Taste of Waking, 2000)

Edith Pedersen

Biographies

Gwyneth Noble

Of Welsh heritage, Gwyneth was born in Ohio but considers Pennsylvania home as it was there she went to Allegheny College, met and married the love of her life, Gene Noble, and raised three sons. Gwyn taught music for fourteen years, volunteered and helped write and present programs for the In-School Program at the Carnegie Museum, as well as volunteering at other arts and community organizations. She and Gene were *gentlemen farmers* at their 120 acre Christmas tree farm in West Virginia, an unforgettable experience that has generated many stories and poems. Since retirement she and her husband divided their lives between Hendersonville, NC, and the Florida Keys before settling permanently and happily in Hendersonville in 2000. They traveled extensively together until Gene's death in 2012.

Always terming herself a word person, Gwyn has used words to journal countless trips, write blurbs, essays, poems, and programs for the many groups with whom she has been associated. After attending a poetry class at the Blue Ridge Community College, she concentrated on that genre. Since then she has published four books of poetry, *The Ladder Holder, a shadowy music, Just a Shadow of Myself,* and *In Love With Shadows* to critical acclaim, finding a wide audience. She has had successful readings in Hendersonville, NC, Pittsburgh, PA, Youngstown, OH, Bainbridge Island, WA, Tucson, AZ, and even on a small tour boat to Alaska. She recently found that poetry has helped her deal with the loss of her husband of sixty-one years and the rebalancing of her life. Words at this time have become both a challenge and a comfort.

Laurabeth "Rusty" Breeding

Rusty's bio begins with childhood on a Canadian farm and settles in the mountains of western North Carolina. Between graduation in 1950 from Pembroke Collegiate and Vocational Institute, Ontario, and retirement from General Electric Company, Hendersonville, NC, her work, in various locations, included clerical, telephone, secretarial and factory.

Joining the Seasoned Poets of the Blue Ridge in 1994 gave her the opportunity to write about the good parts and skip all the hard work, she says. Her poems show an appreciation of nature and of human nature. Sometimes a poem takes hold of itself, she adds, and ends with a wry twist.

Helen Palmer

Helen Palmer taught high school English in Highland Park, Illinois, before retiring in 1989 to Hendersonville, NC. She pursued the usual retiree activities of golf, traveling, bridge, reading, and volunteering. Then in 1994 she joined a poetry group formed through a class at Blue Ridge Community College. Her connection with the Seasoned Poets has kept her writing poetry for twenty years.

Helen writes of daily living–the joys of having pet companions, the seasons' fickleness, the frustrations of dealing with electronics. She looks for humor in life, usually translated into rhymed poems.

Besides appearing in the many anthologies of the Seasoned Poets, Helen published her poetry in *Jigsaw Puzzle* (1997) and *Spilled out of The Jar of Memory* (2003).

Beverly Bryan Russell

Beverly Bryan Russell was born in Gainesville, Georgia, and grew up in suburban Atlanta. She earned her undergraduate degree in English and her M.A. in English Education. Her short story, *Helium Balloon,* won the 1997 Appalachian Regional Writers Award.

A Hendersonville High School English and creative writing teacher, Beverly sponsored the award-winning literary magazine, *Socko.* In 1985 the school system selected her Teacher of the Year.

Beverly has been a member of The Seasoned Poets of the Blue Ridge since her retirement. She published two books of poetry: *Telling Questions* (2002) and *From the Corner of my Eye* (2008).

Beverly contributes a Southern voice to the group, with poems about growing up in the Atlanta area. Her observations of nature and family life are couched in a special kind of music. Like her trout lilies, she approaches the reader with a "shy magic."

Karen Heggen

Karen Heggen has lived in Western NC since 1978. She began writing poems during a year of journaling in 1986. When she met poet Grace Freeman in 1990 Karen began reading contemporary poetry including many women poets. She is heartened that children today are encouraged to write poems. In her childhood most poets seemed to be Englishmen who lived long ago. She remembers no poetry at home except the recording Dylan Thomas made in 1953 during a US tour.

The love of words and the rhythms of speech and song blossomed early in Karen. Her read-aloud, storytelling father made words a game and taught Karen Pig Latin before she started school. High school brought the reading of poetry, a love which lay dormant for decades. Rhetoric and radio announcing held her interest in college. Family history, arts and crafts, and gardening are interests which have informed her poetry in the twenty years the Seasoned Poets have been together. She continues her poetry and her genealogy quest, but today the flowers she admires grow in other people's gardens.

Elda Lepak

photo by Danica Manuel

Elda (Setula) Lepak grew up in central Wisconsin, the fifth of six children in her family. After college, she married Richard, a man who likes to try new things and travel wherever Elda will go. Though spending most of their lives in WI, a ten year break occurred when a job transferred them to NJ, PA, and back to WI.

After their grown children established lives for themselves beyond WI, Richard and Elda retired to NC. Although she is involved in community organizations, plays golf and kayaks, and works on her photography, she is content to squirrel away in her office to write until she is drawn out to join the world.

Thanks to her sister, Linda, and the Seasoned Poets of the Blue Ridge, her writing and publishing of poetry have flourished. Her poems have appeared in the Seasoned Poets of the Blue Ridge Anthologies: *Look Both Ways, A Long and Winding Road, Seasoned Poetry, and Changing Seasons.* Elda's poetry has appeared in *Free Verse, Verse Wisconsin, Wisconsin Poets' Calendars, The Main Street Rag, Song of the San Joaquin,* and the anthology *Empty Shoes: Poems on the Hungry and the Homeless.* She has received awards in poetry contests in WI, NC, and CA.

Her book, *Sky Canvas,* was published in 2010. A book written with her two remaining sisters, Mavis Flegle and Linda Aschbrenner, entitled *Three Sisters from Wisconsin: Our Finnish American Girlhoods with Recollections of Michigan's Upper Peninsula* will be published in 2014.

Anthologies: Seasoned Poets of the Blue Ridge

Beyond Flower Gardens   1994
Apple Country: Hendersonville Poems   1996
Standing On Our Words   1997
Swimming in Stars   1998
The Taste of Waking   2000
Just to the Right of the Moon   2002`
Time Keepers   2006
Look Both Ways   2009
A Long and Winding Road   2011
Seasoned Poetry   2013
Changing Seasons   2014

Titles by the Seasoned Poets of the Blue Ridge

Hazel Herndon Fryer
One Brash Mockingbird   1995
A Handful of Sand   1997
If I Were a Tree   1999
Paper Trail   2001
The Gift of Words   2002

Elda Lepak
Sky Canvas   2010

Gwyneth Owens Noble
The Ladder Holder   1996
A Shadowy Music   1999
Just a Shadow of Myself   2004
In Love with Shadows   2008

Helen Palmer
Jigsaw Puzzle   1997
Spilled out of a Jar of Memory   2003

Edith Pedersen
Where the Wild Grasses Grow   1997

Beverly Bryan Russell
Telling Questions   2002
From the Corner of My Eye   2008

Frances Miner Schneider
Haying Time   1997

Helen van Boer
Wings of the Wind   1998
Walking Backward   2000

32908151R00077

Made in the USA
Charleston, SC
28 August 2014